GET CRAFTY

SPECIAL OCCASIONS

Vivienne Bolton

Editor
Barbara Segall

Art Direction
Full Steam Ahead

DesignTeam
Design Study

Photography
Patrick Spillane

Photographic Co-ordinator
Liz Spillane

Styling
Bianca Boulton

Project Management
Kate Miles

The publishers would like to thank Inscribe Ltd., Bordon, Hants. for
providing the art materials used in these projects and
Sophie Boulton for her assistance.

First published in 1998 by
Dempsey Parr
Queen Street House, 4-5 Queen Street, Bath
BA1 1HE

24681097531

Copyright © Dempsey Parr 1998

Produced by Miles Kelly Publishing Ltd
Unit 11, Bardfield Centre, Great Bardfield, Essex CM7 4SL

British Library Cataloguing-in-Publication Data
A catalogue record for this book is available from the British Library.

ISBN 1-84084-403-5

Printed in Italy

SPECIAL OCCASIONS

Contents

PAPER DRAGON

Chinese New Year

The Chinese New Year is a time when families enjoy reunions and gifts, as with so many of the winter festivals. The story goes that once there was a bad dragon who terrorized the people. The people were very frightened but after a while they discovered that the dragon didn't like loud noises, so they all got together and made lots of loud noises. They banged saucepan lids together, shouted and let off firecrackers to frighten him away. Nowadays there is a grand dragon procession with fireworks and many people holding up a giant paper dragon. After the event families join together to eat specially prepared meals to welcome in the New Year. They give gifts of money wrapped in red envelopes to each other. The Chinese New Year begins with a new moon, and it is also the time when the farmers gave thanks for the harvest. Have fun making your own small Chinese dragon and if there are a few of you, why not make lots of dragons so you can have your own Chinese New Year procession.

You will need:

Thin cardboard

Felt-tip pens

Glitter

Glue

Scissors

Tissue paper

Paper

Tape

Two sticks

1 Draw a dragon's head onto a piece of thin cardboard. Use felt-tip pens to color and decorate it with glitter.

4 Make the body by taking two strips of paper and folding them one over the other repeatedly to make a concertina.

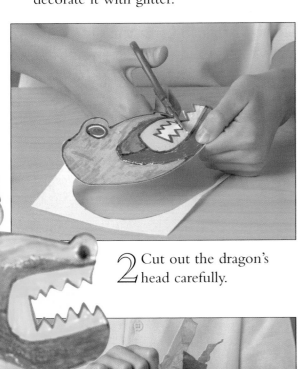

2 Cut out the dragon's head carefully.

5 Attach paper ribbons to the dragon's tail. Glue the head to the other end of the body.

3 Cut strips of tissue paper to use as ribbons. Use the glue to stick these paper ribbons to the dragon's head.

6 Use sticky tape to attach the sticks to the dragon's body. One is for the head and the other for the tail.

St. Valentine's Day

You will need a heart-shaped cookie cutter to make both the picture frames and the gingerbread hearts! Both will make great Valentine gifts to give to friends and sweethearts. The gingerbread cookies are simple to make and can be decorated with frosting or left plain.

Either way they are delicious to eat. The heart-shaped picture frame has space for two pictures. It is made by rolling out the clay and using two cookie cutters to cut the frame, one smaller than the other. A coat of varnish (or clear nail polish) will give your picture frame a professional finish.

You will need:

Air-hardening clay
Heart cookie cutter
Red paint
Paintbrush
Thread or ribbon
Glue

Recipe for gingerbread biscuits

2 1/3 cups plain flour

1 teaspoon baking powder

2 teaspoons ground ginger

1 teaspoon cinnamon

1 stick margarine

1 cup soft brown sugar

3 tablespoons syrup

1 egg

Frosting

1 Place the flour, baking powder, ginger, cinnamon, and sugar in a large bowl. Add the margarine, mix it in well with your fingertips until the mixture looks crumbly like breadcrumbs.

2 Add the sugar and syrup; mix together. Use a spoon to stir in the egg and mix.

3 Turn the mixture out onto the work surface and knead the mixture until it is smooth and well mixed. Sprinkle some flour onto the work surface and use the rolling pin to roll the mixture out to a thickness of about one quarter of an inch. With a heart-shaped cookies cutter cut out the shapes. Place the shapes on a baking tray and bake at 325°F for just 10 minutes. Get an adult to help you use the oven.

4 When the gingerbread cookies are cooked take them out of the oven and leave to stand until cold. They will harden up as they cool. When they are cool, decorate the cookies with frosting.

5 To make these picture frames you will need two cookie cutters, one smaller than the other, and some air-hardening clay. Roll out the clay and cut out two large heart shapes. One of the heart shapes will be the picture frame back. Take the smaller heart-shaped cookie cutter and cut a small heart shape out of the second heart shape. Leave the made frame pieces to dry in a warm airy place. When they have dried completely, paint them with red paint and glue them together. Place a picture of your Valentine in the frame. Use glue to secure it to the frame.

The heart-shaped frames look good enough to eat, but remember they are made from air-hardening clay and are not edible!

PHOTO WALLET
Mother's Day

ake your mother this pretty photo wallet for Mother's Day. It is made with card and attractive handmade paper, but would be equally good made with decorated paper or covered with a printed fabric. A photograph of you when you were a baby would make a good cover picture rather than the cut-out flower. If you have brothers and sisters put photographs of all of you in the wallet. Use your imagination and the materials you have in your scrap box to come up with something good.

You will need:

Scissors

Paper

Cardboard

Glue

Ribbon

Pictures

Photographs

1 You will need two equal sized pieces of thick cardboard for the cover. Glue them onto attractive handmade paper.

4 Glue a piece of ribbon to the inside of both cardboard covers. This will tie in a pretty bow to keep your wallet closed.

2 Fold the handmade paper in neatly and firmly, then glue it securely down, so that the outer edges of the two pieces of cardboard are completely covered.

5 Stick one end of the folded page section to the inside front cover. It should cover the ribbon end too. Fix the other end of the page section to the inside back cover.

3 Now take a long piece of handmade paper and make a concertina fold. This will make the pages of the wallet.

6 Decorate the front cover with ribbon and a cutout picture of flowers, or maybe use a picture of yourself .

GIFTS, CARDS, AND DECORATIONS
Easter

In the Northern Hemisphere Easter occurs in the springtime, so we have Easter bunnies, eggs, and spring flowers, such as the daffodils on this delightful Easter card. It is fun to make and grandparents will enjoy receiving greeting cards at this time of year. The chocolate nests are made from breakfast cereal and melted chocolate. The tiny eggs are chocolate covered raisins, or, instead, you could use small foil covered chocolate Easter eggs. Another fun Easter activity is to make an Easter tree. This tree is made from a branch decorated with paper Easter eggs.

You will need:

Shredded breakfast cereal

Bowl

Melted chocolate

Spoon

Foil

Muffin pan

Chocolate covered raisins

1 Crumble the cereal by hand into a bowl. Check that there are no large chunks.

2 Carefully add the melted chocolate to the bowl of crumbled cereal and, using the spoon, mix well together.

3 Line a muffin pan with foil and place a spoonful of the mixture into each space. Use the back of the spoon to press it down into a nest shape. Leave the shapes to harden in a cool, dry place.

4 When the nests are hard, put them on a plate and add a few chocolate covered raisins to each one. Serve up as a treat on Easter Sunday.

5 A branch decorated with paper Easter eggs will brighten up the home. Cut the Easter eggs from paper and decorate them using pencil crayons. Make a hole at one end of each egg and thread with string to hang them on the Easter tree.

6 Use colored paper to make this Easter card. The daffodils have bright yellow paper petals and a paler yellow center. Cut the leaves from green paper. Use glue to attach the flowers to the card.

PAPERWEIGHTS
Father's Day

This useful paperweight should be a great success as a gift on Father's Day. You will need a wooden doorknob or other small, but weighty, object to decorate. Choose a decoration that will suit his personality or hobbies; a garden-loving father would enjoy the gardening design and a handyman would like the woodworking tools! If he plays golf you could stick a real golf ball and tee onto the paperweight. Paint the paperweight in colors that suit the decoration—greens and browns for gardening or maybe blue, if your decoration has a watery theme.

You will need:
Wooden doorknob

Oven-bake clay

Glue

Paintbrush

Paint

Varnish

Small decorations could be made from air-hardening clay and painted if you did not have any oven-bake clay.

1 Use colored oven-bake clay to make the vegetables. The carrots are made from tiny sausage shapes thinned at one end with a few green pieces stuck on as stalks. To make the cabbages begin with a few small ball shapes, and flatten them into leaf shapes. When you have made a few leaves press them, one by one, onto a small ball, until you have a hearty-looking cabbage. Pumpkins are made from flattened ball shapes, and the tomatoes are small red ball shapes with tiny green stalks. The miniature basket came from a florist's shop, but you could make a basket from clay. Harden the vegetables in the oven according to the manufacturer's instructions. Paint the doorknob dark green. Use strong glue to attach the vegetables and basket to the doorknob.

3 The doorknob has been left unpainted for this carpenter's design. Make the miniature tools from oven-bake clay, baked in the oven according to the manufacturer's instructions.

4 Use glue to attach the hardened tools to the doorknob and when the glue has dried, varnish the paperweight. For a golfing father, decorate the doorknob with a golf ball and tee.

2 When the glue has dried brighten up the paperweight with a little red paint and then varnish the whole item to give a professional finish.

HOMEMADE SOUP AND BREAD
Harvest Supper

Harvest is a special time of year. It comes at the end of summer when the farmers have harvested all the summer grown crops, ready to store for winter use. After harvest, wheat is ground into flour for bread and the kitchens of vegetable gardeners are full to overflowing. We have prepared a pot of soup using a mixture of seasonal vegetables and made some bread rolls and a loaf to enjoy with the soup. Ask an adult to supervise the cooking and make a special family harvest supper.

You will need:
A package of bread mix

Bowl

A little extra flour

Baking tray

Egg

Pastry brush

Rack

Soup ingredients

Knife

Large saucepan and water

Fork

Small soup bowl

Soup recipe:

1 onion

2 sticks of celery

2 medium potatoes

2 large carrots

1 leek

A vegetable stock cube

1 teaspoon of mixed herbs

A squeeze of tomato paste

A little oil

Salt and pepper to taste

Always check with an adult before using the oven.

1 Follow the directions on the bread mix package. You will need to pour the package mix into a bowl and add the required quantity of water. Mix well with a spoon until the mixture forms a dough.

2 Sprinkle the work surface with a little flour. Empty the dough onto the work surface and use your hands to knead it. After a few minutes you will see and feel that the dough becomes smooth. When it is all smooth to touch and eye, you can begin to shape it.

3 Divide it in two sections and shape it into bread rolls and a plaited loaf. Place them on a baking tray. Brush with beaten egg and leave in a warm spot to rise. When the dough has doubled in size, bake according to the instructions on the package.

4 When the bread is ready it will smell delicious and be a lovely golden brown color. Ask an adult to help take the bread out of the oven. Place the cooked bread on a rack to cool.

5 Chop up the vegetables before you begin to make the soup. Place all the ingredients into a large saucepan. Pour enough water into the saucepan to cover the ingredients. Bring to the boil and then turn down the heat so the soup cooks gently. Allow to cook for half an hour.

6 Ask an adult to help. Prick some of the vegetables with a fork to make sure they are cooked. Season with salt and pepper if necessary. Serve in a small soup bowl and enjoy your soup with your freshly baked harvest bread and rolls.

SAND AND PETAL PICTURE
Diwali

Followers of the Hindu religion celebrate many festivals. Diwali, or the Festival of Light, is my favorite Hindu festival. Diwali is celebrated around October/November time and is a New Year celebration. In Hindu homes the house is cleaned and decorated with colored glitter, sand, and flowers. Lots of small clay lamps are kept burning on windowsills and on doorsteps. These lights are to welcome Lakshmi, the goddess of wealth. Everyone hopes she will visit them over this period and bring good fortune for the New Year. Many Hindu homes in India have sand pictures drawn up outside their front doors to welcome visitors. Make a sand and flower picture to place in your hall during Diwali.

You will need:

Air-hardening clay

Paintbrush and paint

Paper and pencil

Glue stick

Colored sand

Flower petals

Glitter

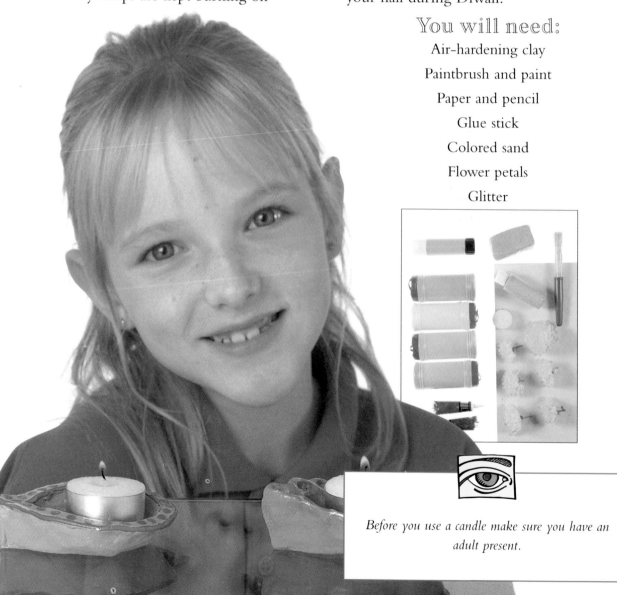

Before you use a candle make sure you have an adult present.

1 To make your Diwali lamp you will need a ball of air-hardening clay. Use your fingers to shape it into a bowl shape and press a fancy edge into the clay. When the lamp has dried, paint it in bright colors and decorate with gold or silver paint. Place a nightlight candle in the lamp and check with an adult before you light it.

2 You will need a large piece of paper. Use a pencil to sketch a flower picture onto the paper. Use a glue stick to mark the centre of the flower.

3 Pour colored sand onto the glue mark.

4 Next use the glue stick to mark out the shape of the petals.

5 Pour colored sand onto the glue lines.

6 When you have completed the sand picture place flower petals as a border.

8 Use glitter to add the finishing touch to your Diwali picture.

LANTERNS, GAMES, AND CREATURES
Halloween

Halloween is a spooky time of year. Make a hollowed-out pumpkin lantern. Carve a face on one side of the pumpkin and stand it outside your home with a lit candle inside. The golden candle light will shine through the dark! For ghoulish fun try making this very squidgy Halloween game. Your friends will enjoy plenty of laughs searching the green gunge for spiders and worms. The glow-in-the-dark character worm is made from oven-bake glow clay. You could make some to put in trick or treat boxes. Open them in the dark to enjoy the glow!

1 Half fill a large bowl with water. Add enough food coloring to turn the water dark green. Sprinkle 3 or 4 tablespoons of wallpaper glue onto the water. Allow the wallpaper glue to sink to the bottom and then stir gently with the spoon until the mixture is sloppy and thick.

2 Add the spiders and toads and the game is ready to play. Take turns to feel through the gunge and guess which creature you are fishing out.

3 Make the cute little glow-in-the-dark worm with special oven-bake glow clay. Make the body first, then form it into the worm shape. Make a number of small ball shapes in dark green and flatten them. Press them onto the worm. Make a hat and place it on the worm's head. Bake the completed model according to the manufacturer's instructions. You could stand the finished worm on a shelf as an ornament or turn him into a fridge magnet or brooch.

You will need:
Bowl

Water

Green food coloring

Wallpaper glue

A selection of plastic toads and spiders

Oven-bake glow clay

Pumpkin

Knife

Candle

FESTIVAL CANDLESTICK
Hanukkah

Hanukkah is the Jewish festival of lights. It is celebrated as a reminder of the time 2,000 years ago when the Jewish Temple was destroyed in battle by the Syrian king. When the battle was over the Jewish people repaired the Temple and went to light the oil lamp which burns in front of the Ark. They found they had hardly any oil, only enough for one day. But, by a miracle, the oil lasted eight days, long enough for the people to prepare more Holy oil to burn. Nowadays Jewish families celebrate Hanukkah in December for eight days, lighting a candle each day until they are all lit. Then they enjoy a time of celebration with parties, games and gifts. You can make a small Hanukkah candlestick to stand on a windowsill. Keep it lit through the festival.

1 Divide your clay into thirds. Roll two thirds out into a long rectangle. Cut out a zigzag pattern to make the base of the candlestick. Flatten the edges of the zigzag so that the candlestick will stand securely.

The remaining third of the clay will make the candleholders. You will need one candleholder in the center and four on each side of it.

2 Assemble the candlestick and leave it in a dry, warm, airy place before decorating it.

3 The candlestick is decorated with paint and glitter. Ask an adult to help each day. First light the center candle and use that to light the other candles day by day. On the first day light one candle, on the second light two candles and so on, until the eighth when all eight candles will be lit.

You will need:

Air-hardening clay

Modeling tool

Paint

Paintbrush

Glitter

Candles

Advent

The twenty-four days before Christmas are marked by an Advent calendar. This calendar is made from a sheet of painted chipboard. Hammer twenty-four tacks into the decorated board and on each tack hang a small gift. You can fill small boxes with a mixture of homemade gifts and bought trinkets. Chocolate or other candies would be suitable Advent gifts to wrap and hang up on the calendar. You might want to make an Advent calendar for a younger brother or sister to hang in their own room as sharing the treats may be difficult!

1 Paint one side of the chipboard a rich dark blue. It may need more than one coat.

2 Use a sponge dipped in silver paint to decorate the edges of the board.

3 Cut a star shape from the center of a piece of paper and use it as a stencil. Use the sponge and silver paint to stencil stars attractively across the blue painted board.

4 Hammer twenty-four tacks into the board. Space them out evenly.

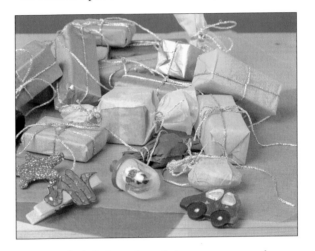

5 Use brightly colored tissue paper and gold thread to wrap up all twenty-four small gifts you have collected. Hang the gifts up on the board and your Advent calendar is ready to use.

You will need:

Piece of chipboard

Paint and paintbrush

Sponge and saucer

Paper

Scissors

Hammer and 24 tacks

Small gifts

Tissue paper

Gold thread

TREE DECORATIONS
Christmas Time

When the Christmas tree goes up we know Christmas is definitely on the way. Presents will soon be piling up underneath it and excitement is in the air. Spend an afternoon making some of these decorations to hang on your tree. You can use card and paper, glitter and string to make these keepsake decorations. The tiny angels are made from rice and pasta shapes, glued together and painted gold. They are quite easy for even tiny hands to make.

If you do not have glitter glue, make your own. Use strong white glue and mix in an equal amount of fine glitter.

24

1 Use strong glue to stick the pasta shapes together. Begin with a quill shape, this will be the angel body. A bow shape will make the angel wings, glue this onto the quill. Glue a wooden ball on as a head and a few grains of rice as hair, and a loop of thread to hang the angel onto the tree. When the glue has dried firmly, decorate the angel with gold paint.

3 Save some poppy seedpods in the summer. Dry them and when Christmas comes round turn them into beautiful baubles. Cut away the stems and glue on a loop of gold thread to hang the decoration onto the tree. Paint the seedhead gold and when dry you will have a lovely tree decoration.

2 This shower of gold stars looks very pretty hanging on the Christmas tree. Cut star shapes from gold tissue paper or plain paper painted gold. Glue the stars onto long pieces of gold thread and then drape them over the Christmas tree. These stars would also look good draped across the mantlepiece, shimmering in the light.

4 These colorful baubles are cut out of thin metallic cardboard. Use a paper punch to make a hole for the loop of thread and decorate the baubles with strips of metallic cardboard and glitter.

Christmas Eve

A small Nativity scene looks beautiful set up on the mantlepiece at Christmas time and reminds us of the wonderful story of Jesus' birth. This miniature scene is made from air-hardening clay. The shapes are all very simple and each piece is painted carefully to create the characters. The stable is made from clay but you might want to decorate a small box as the stable and then use the box to store the Nativity scene when not on display. A Nativity scene would make a thoughtful gift for grandparents. You could keep it to use again next year.

You will need:

Air-hardening clay

Paint

Paintbrushes

Gold glitter

Varnish

1 Begin by shaping the stable from a ball of clay. Next make a small cradle to hold Baby Jesus. Make a small baby shape and place it in the cradle. Mary and Joseph will be next; make Joseph a little larger than Mary. You will need a few shepherds and some shapes for sheep. Make sure these will stand up on their own. Make the three wise men last. Leave all the clay pieces to dry in a warm airy spot, then you can decorate them.

2 Follow the illustration above when painting your Nativity scene. Mary will need to have a blue cloak, and the three wise men should have a bit of gold glitter sparkling on them somewhere. Paint the sheep white with black faces and legs. When the scene is all painted allow the pieces to dry, then varnish them.

3 Joseph, Mary, and Baby Jesus in the manger: a Christmas scene to remind us of the real reason behind Christmas.

CRACKERS
Christmas Day

Home made Christmas crackers are one of the many things you can make in advance in preparation for Christmas. Fill them with paper hats, jokes (good ones!) and small gifts which you could make, such as necklaces or small brooches or badges. Paper hats are easy to make from tissue paper. You will need to fold them up small so they fit in the crackers. The snaps are available from craft shops. You might want to make a special cracker for a grandparent or friend you won't be seeing over the Christmas season. Send it to them through the post so that they can pull it while they are enjoying their Christmas dinner.

You will need:

Tissue paper, for hat and cracker

Scissors

Thin cardboard

Sticky tape

Small gift to put inside the cracker

Snaps

Glue

Glitter

You could use the central cardboard cylinder from a roll of toilet paper to shape your crackers.

1 Before you make the cracker you will need to make a tissue paper hat. Use your own head to make a standard size hat. If you are making the hat to fit an adult-head, make it a little larger. Cut a zigzag shape along one side, and glue the two short edges together.

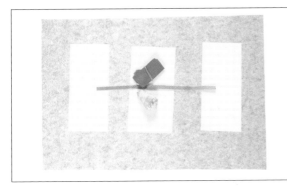

2 To make the cracker you will need a sheet of tissue paper measuring 16 in. x 8 in. and three pieces of thin cardboard 7 in. x 4 in. Add a snap, a paper hat tightly folded, and a small gift.

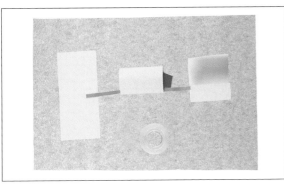

3 Roll the pieces of thin cardboard into cylinder shapes. Hold them in place with tape. Run the snap through the cylinders and place the hat and gift in the central cylinder.

4 Roll the tissue paper around the cylinders and use thread to tie in between them. Pull up the thread firmly to create the cracker shape. Remove the two end cylinders and trim any excess paper away.

5 The cracker is ready to decorate. Use glitter and glue on a seasonal picture.

CAKES

Special Days

These novelty cakes look great on a party table and would make a surprise birthday gift to take to a party. The frosting is simply rolled out with a rolling pin then placed over the cake. The decorative pieces are cut using cookie cutters which come in so many shapes and sizes you are sure to find one to suit the style of cake you want to make. Use a bought-in sponge cake to ice or make your own following the easy recipe below. Ask an adult for help when you use the oven.

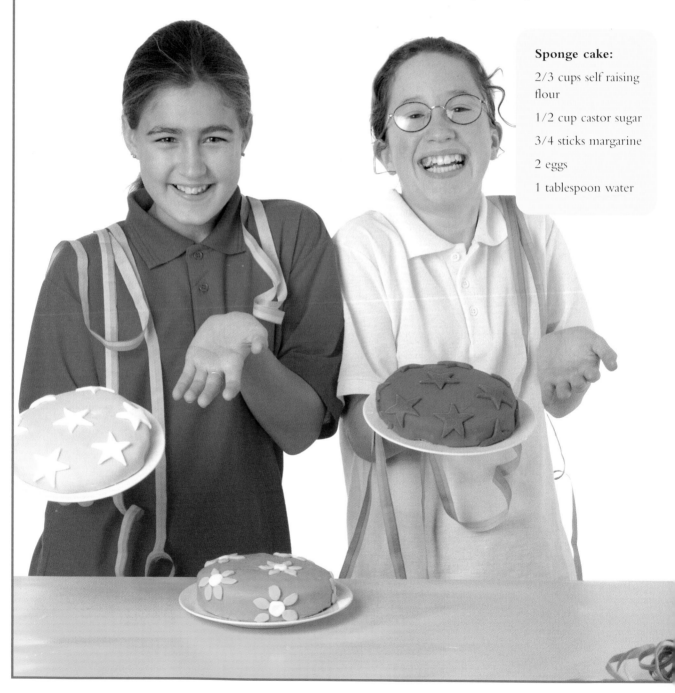

Sponge cake:

2/3 cups self raising flour

1/2 cup castor sugar

3/4 sticks margarine

2 eggs

1 tablespoon water

1 Sieve some superfine sugar onto your work surface so that the frosting doesn't stick to it and roll out the frosting to about a quarter inch thickness.

2 Roll the frosting over the rolling pin and, lifting it gently, transfer it to the cake. Drape it over the cake and carefully remove the rolling pin.

3 Gently press the frosting over the cake. Cut away any excess frosting with a knife. Use a clean cloth to wipe away any frosting sugar.

4 Roll out some red frosting and use a cookie cutter to cut out the star shapes. Moisten the back of the stars with water and press them gently onto the cake.

5 Use different shaped cookie cutters to create different styles of cake. Green frogs, red stars, or blue fish could be cut out and decorated further with silver balls or edible felt-tip colors. Have fun creating your own designs to suit different occasions.

You will need

Sponge cakes to frost

Superfine sugar

Rolling pin

Easy-roll frosting

Knife

Clean cloth

Small sieve

Cookie cutters

A little water and a pastry brush

Index

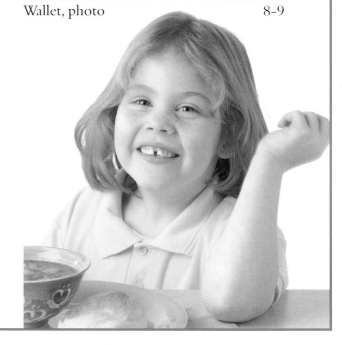